T0050789

Accelerando

Accelerando

becoming faster

Accidental

Accidental

a sharp or flat not given
in the key signature

Alla marcia

Alla marcia

like a march

Animato

Animato

spirited, with energy

A tempo

A tempo

return to the original speed

Allegretto

Allegretto

lively, but slower than allegro

Cantabile

Cantabile

singing

Con moto

Con moto

with motion

D.C. al Coda

D.C. al Coda

Return to the beginning (capo)
and play until the first coda sign
⊕ then skip to the next coda sign.

D.S. al Fine

Del Segno al Fine

Return to the segno sign 𝄋
and play to the end (fine).

Dim.

Diminuendo

gradually softer

Dolce

Dolce

sweetly

Dynamics

Dynamics

how loud or soft to play

Expressivo

Espressivo

with feeling

Grazioso

Grazioso

gracefully

Giocoso

Giocoso

humorously

Harmonic
Interval

Harmonic Interval

the distance between two notes
played at the same time

Interval

Interval

the distance between two pitches

Largo

Largo

very slowly

Lento

Lento

slowly

Loco

Loco

play the notes where written

Maestoso

Maestoso

majestically

Melodic
Interval

Melodic Interval

the distance between two notes
played one after the other

Meno

Meno

less

Moderato

Moderato

moderate tempo

Molto

Molto

much

Piu

Piu

more

Poco

Poco

a little bit

Portamento

slightly disconnected

Presto

Presto

fast

Prestissimo

Prestissimo

faster than Presto; the fastest tempo

Scherzando

Scherzando

playfully

Sempre

Sempre

always

Simile

Simile

in a similar way

Sostenuto

Sostenuto

sustained

Tempo

Tempo

rate of speed

Tenuto

hold the note for its full value

Upbeat

Upbeat

note(s) that come before
the first full measure

Vivace

Vivace

lively, brisk, bright

Vivo

Vivo

lively

Patterns, Scales, and Chord Progressions
help students recognize fundamental harmonies in major and relative minor key centers.

The white cards in *Set B*, numbered 41-80, include a description and display a total of ***39 different musical examples*** in the following keys:

C Major	–	A Minor
G Major	–	E Minor
F Major	–	D Minor

Activities:

1) *Teacher displays the musical example and student identifies.*

2) *Teacher displays only the "answer" and student plays the example on the piano.*

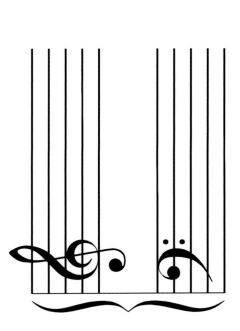

What is the
Major Key?

What is the
Minor Key?

What is the Key Signature?

C Major   A Minor

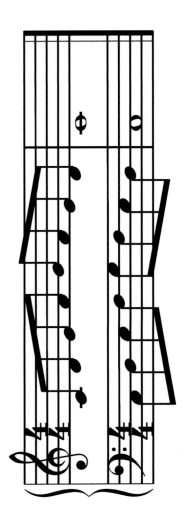

C Major Five-Finger Pattern

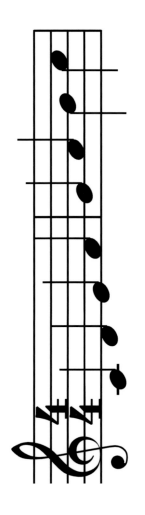

C Major Scale

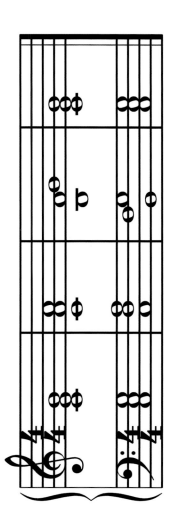

C Major Chord Progression
I - IV - V7 - I

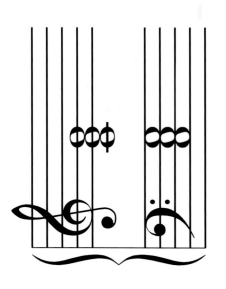

Name the root.

The root is C.

C Major Chord
(I of C Major)

Name the root.

The root is F.

F Major Chord
(IV of C Major)

Name the root.

The root is G.

G7 Chord
(V7 of C Major)

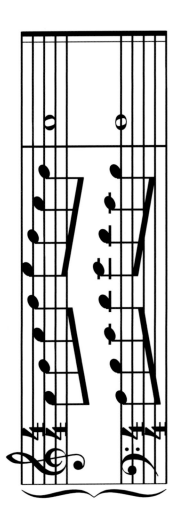

A Minor Five-Finger Pattern

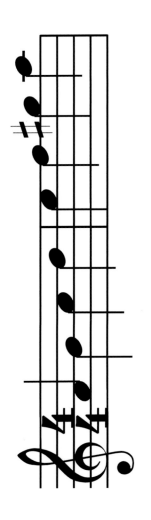

A Minor Scale
(Harmonic)

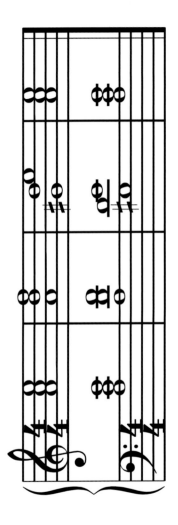

A Minor Chord Progression
i - iv - V7 - i

Name the root.

The root is A.

A Minor Chord
(i of A Minor)

Name the root.

The root is D.

D Minor Chord
(iv of A Minor)

Name the root.

The root is E.

E7 Chord
(V7 of A Minor)

What is the
Major Key?

What is the
Minor Key?

What is the Key Signature?

G Major   E Minor

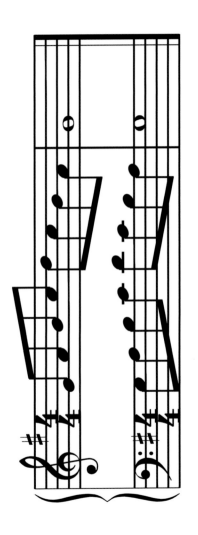

G Major Five-Finger Pattern

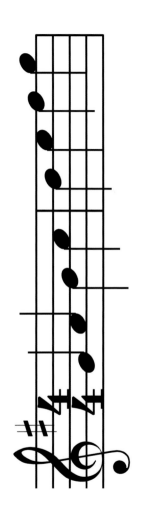

G Major Scale

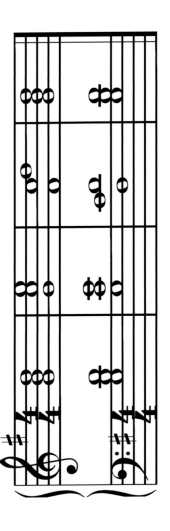

G Major Chord Progression
I - IV - V7 - I

Name the root.

The root is G.

G Major Chord
(I of G Major)

Name the root.

The root is C.

C Major Chord
(IV of G Major)

Name the root.

The root is D.

D7 Chord
(V7 of G Major)

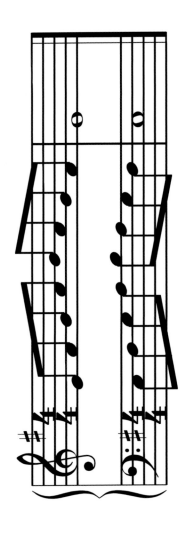

E Minor Five-Finger Pattern

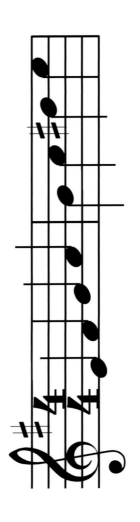

E Minor Scale
(Harmonic)

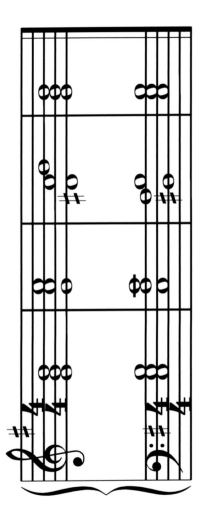

E Minor Chord Progression
i - iv - V7 - i

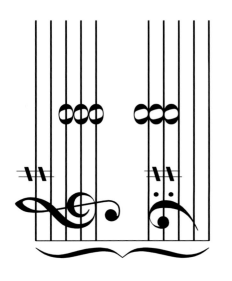

Name the root.

The root is E.

E Minor Chord
(i of E Minor)

Name the root.

The root is A.

A Minor Chord
(iv of E Minor)

Name the root.

The root is B.

B7 Chord
(V7 of E Minor)

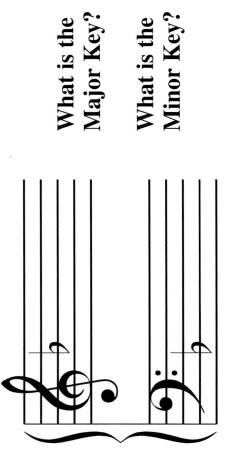

What is the Major Key?

What is the Minor Key?

What is the Key Signature?

F Major   D Minor

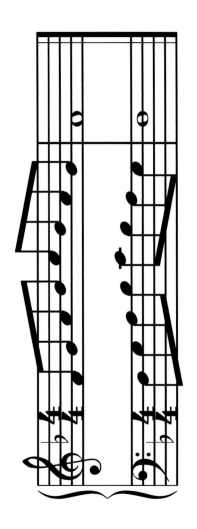

F Major Five-Finger Pattern

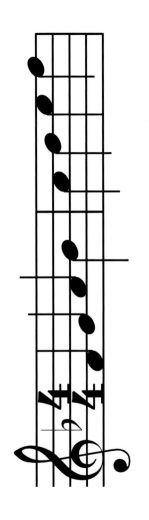

F Major Scale

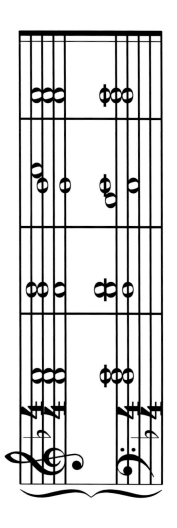

F Major Chord Progression
I - IV - V7 - I

Name the root.

The root is F.

F Major Chord
(I of F Major)

Name the root.

The root is B♭.

B♭ Major Chord
(IV of F Major)

Name the root.

The root is C.

C7 Chord
(V7 of F Major)

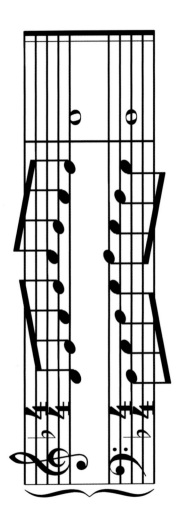

D Minor Five-Finger Pattern

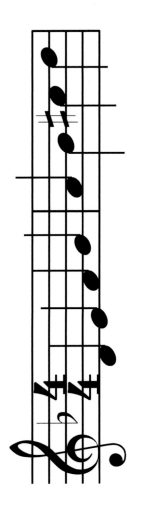

D Minor Scale
(Harmonic)

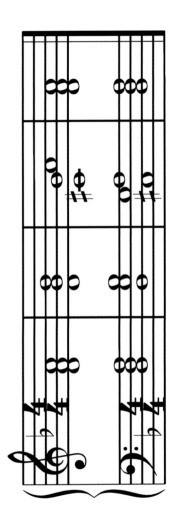

D Minor Chord Progression
i - iv - V7 - i

Name the root.

The root is D.

D Minor Chord
(i of D Minor)

Name the root.

The root is G.

G Minor Chord
(iv of D Minor)

Name the root.

The root is A.

A7 Chord
(V7 of D Minor)

Rhythm Reading Cards
encourage students to read rhythm
patterns in four-measure phrases.

The yellow cards in *Set B,* numbered
52-80, display a total of **58 different rhythm patterns** which can be
taught by:

1) clapping hands
2) tapping knees
3) playing a percussive instrument
4) playing a single key on the piano

Note and Rest Values used in *Set B:*

Time Signatures used in *Set B:*

$\frac{4}{4}$ $\frac{3}{4}$ $\frac{2}{4}$ $\frac{3}{8}$ $\frac{6}{8}$ **C** **₵**

Activities (over)

Rhythm Card Activities

1) *The student sets the tempo by counting an introductory measure(s), then claps and counts Rhythm Card.*

2) *The teacher displays the Rhythm Cards side-by-side on the music rack. Each time the student repeats a two-card rhythm pattern, the teacher replaces the second card with a new rhythm.*

3) *Once the student has mastered several Rhythm Cards, the teacher displays one card after another while the student claps each new rhythm without skipping a beat between patterns. For a challenge, mix different time signatures.*

4) *Set the metronome and count the Rhythm Cards at slower or faster tempos.*

5) *The teacher displays two or more Rhythm Cards on the music rack and claps one. The student selects the correct pattern.*

TWO EIGHTH NOTES

fill the time of one quarter note

1 Count in 2/4, 3/4, or 4/4;
2 Counts in 3/8 or 6/8

EIGHTH NOTE

fills <u>half</u> the time of
one quarter note

1/2 Count in 2/4, 3/4, or 4/4;
1 Count in 3/8 or 6/8

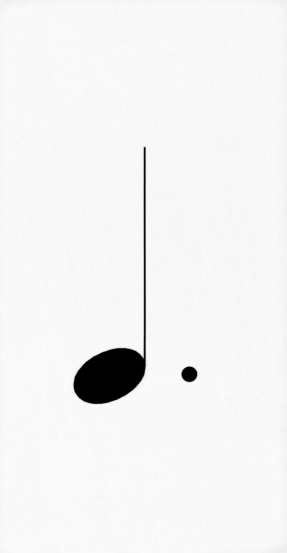

DOTTED QUARTER NOTE

fills the time of three eighth notes

1 & 1/2 Counts in 2/4, 3/4, or 4/4;
3 Counts in 3/8 or 6/8

EIGHTH REST

fills the time of one eighth note

1/2 Count in 2/4, 3/4, or 4/4;
1 Count in 3/8 or 6/8

EIGHTH NOTE TRIPLET

fills the time of one quarter note

1 Count

24

TIME SIGNATURE

$$\frac{2}{4}$$

2 = two beats fill each measure

♩ = quarter note gets one beat

38

TIME SIGNATURE

3 = three beats fill each measure
♪ = eighth note gets one beat

68

TIME SIGNATURE

$$\frac{6}{8}$$

6 = six beats fill each measure

♪ = eighth note gets one beat

COMMON TIME

c

another name for $\frac{4}{4}$

$\mathbf{c} \begin{pmatrix} 4 \\ \end{pmatrix}$ = four beats fill each measure
= quarter note gets one beat

CUT TIME

$\mathbb{C} \left(\genfrac{}{}{0pt}{}{2}{\text{♩}} \right)$ = two beats fill each measure
= half note gets one beat

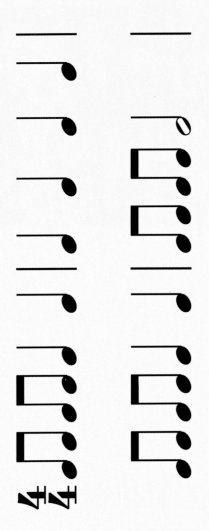

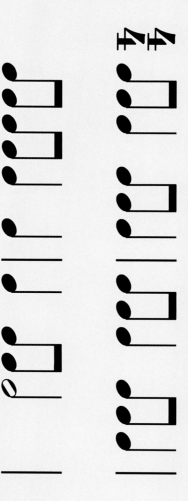

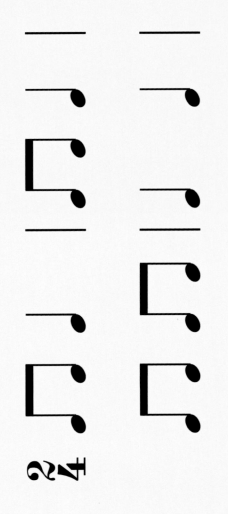

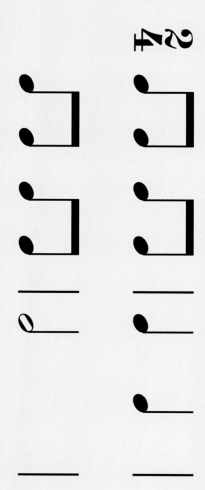

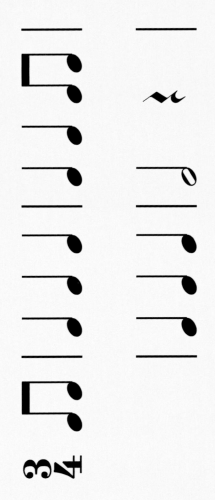

54

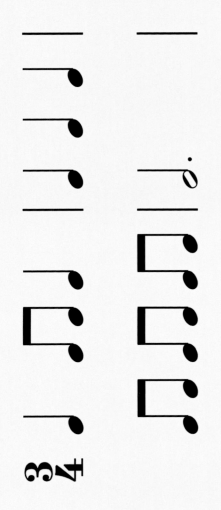

55

© Hal Leonard

Swing eighths

Swing eighths

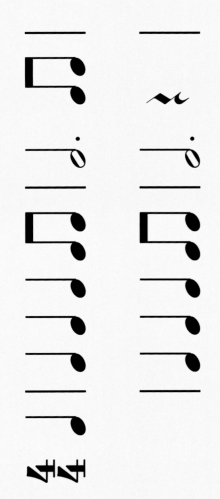

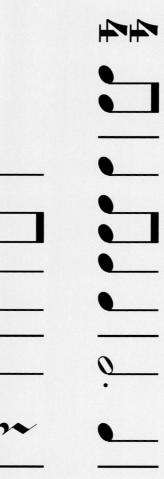

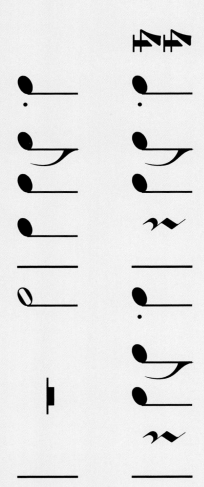

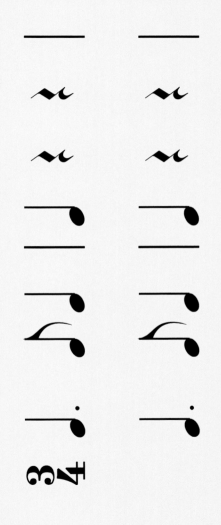

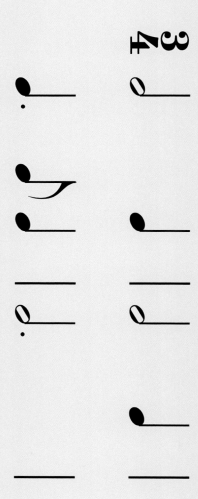

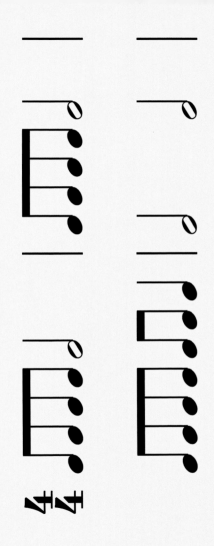

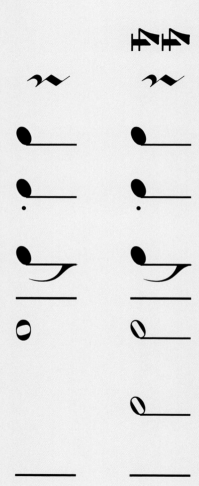

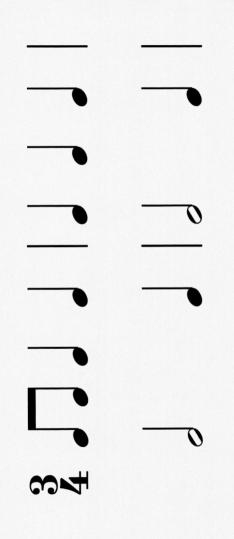

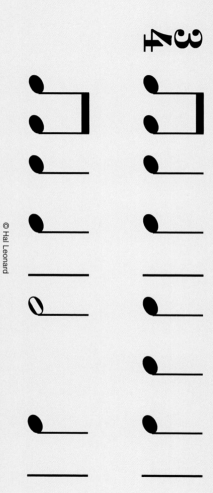

61

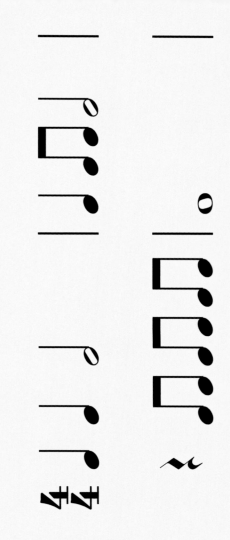

63

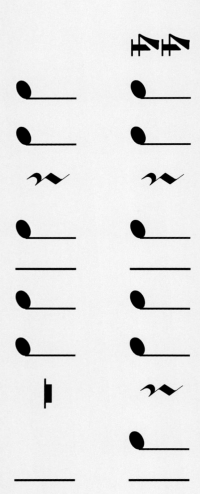

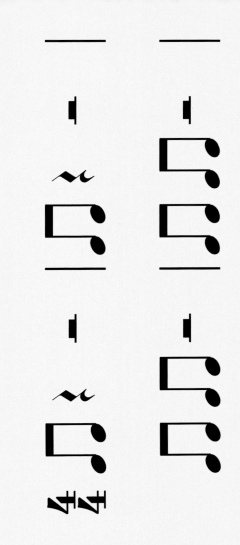

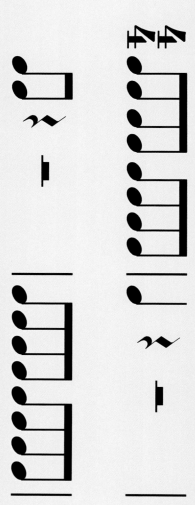

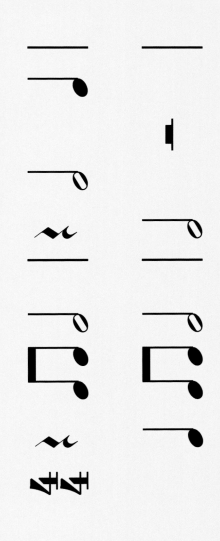

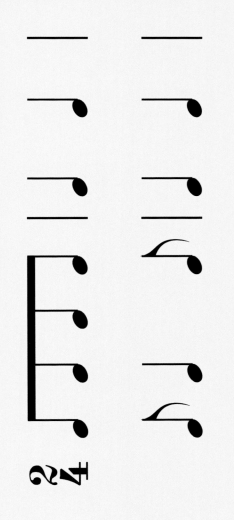

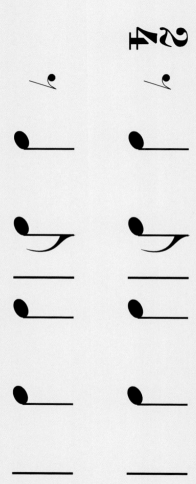

80

© Hal Leonard

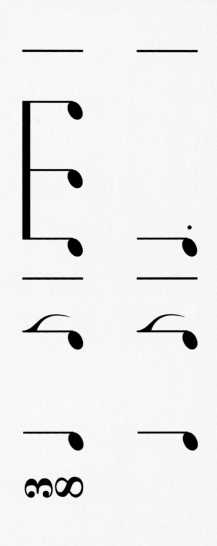

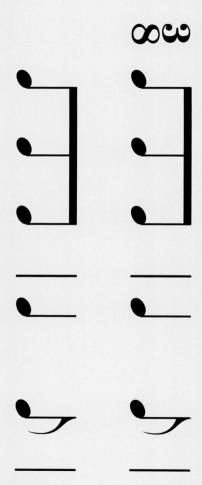

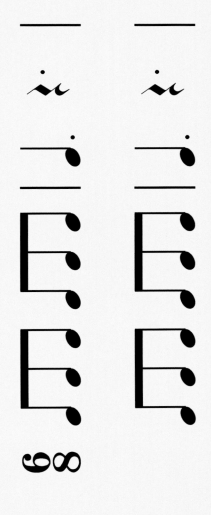

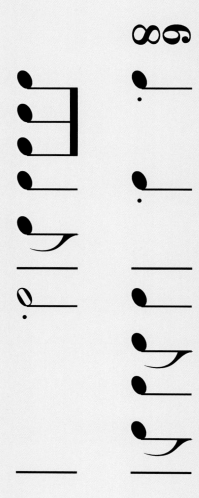

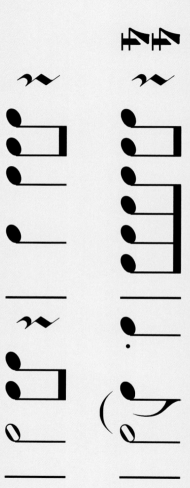

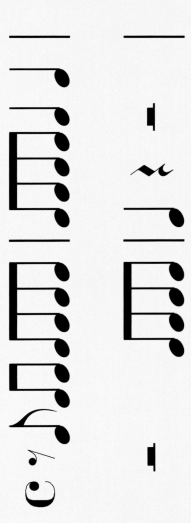

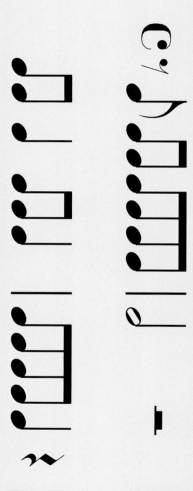

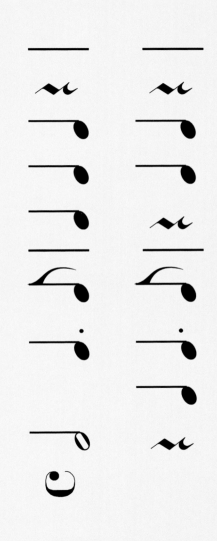

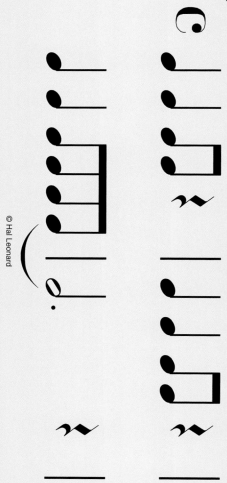

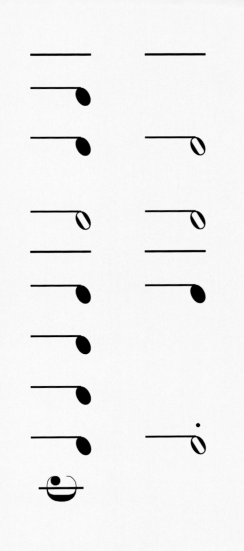

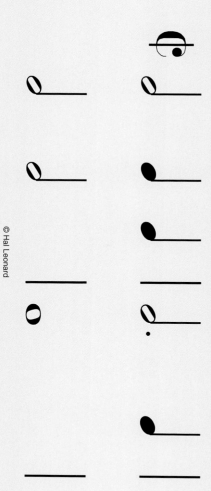

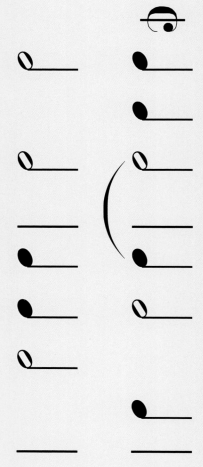

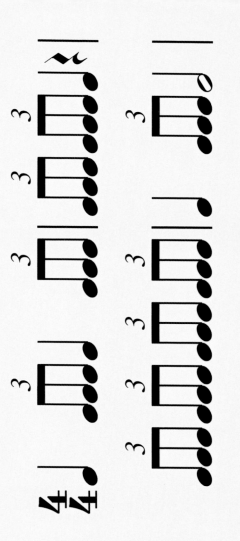

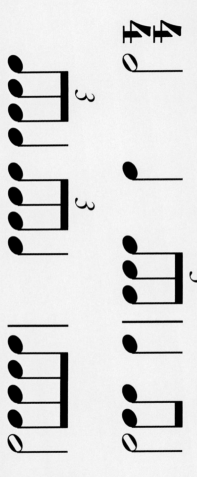

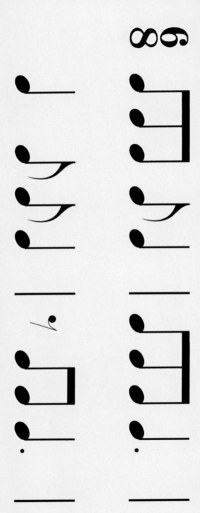

TWO QUAVER NOTES

fill the time of one crotchet note

1 Count in 2/4, 3/4, or 4/4;
2 Counts in 3/8 or 6/8

QUAVER NOTE

fills <u>half</u> the time of
one crotchet note

1/2 Count in 2/4, 3/4, or 4/4;
1 Count in 3/8 or 6/8

DOTTED CROTCHET NOTE

fills the time of three quaver notes

1 & 1/2 Counts in 2/4, 3/4, or 4/4;
3 Counts in 3/8 or 6/8

QUAVER REST

fills the time of one quaver note

1/2 Count in 2/4, 3/4, or 4/4;
1 Count in 3/8 or 6/8

QUAVER NOTE TRIPLET

fills the time of one crotchet note

1 Count

24

TIME SIGNATURE

$\frac{2}{4}$

2 = two beats fill each bar

♩ = crotchet note gets one beat

38

TIME SIGNATURE

3
8

3 = three beats fill each bar

♪ = quaver note gets one beat

68

TIME SIGNATURE

$$\frac{6}{8}$$

6 = six beats fill each bar

♪ = quaver note gets one beat

C

COMMON TIME

C

another name for $\frac{4}{4}$

c $\left(\begin{array}{c}4\\ \text{♩}\end{array}\right)$ = four beats fill each bar
= crotchet note gets one beat

CUT COMMON TIME

¢ $\left(\begin{array}{c}2\\ \text{♩}\end{array}\right)$ = two beats fill each bar
= minim note gets one beat

Swing quavers

Swing quavers